The Story of
Clara Barton

by Rachel A. Koestler-Grack

CHELSEA
Philadelphia

Chelsea Clubhouse books are published by Chelsea House Publishers,
a subsidiary of Haights Cross Communications.

A Haights Cross Communications Company

The Chelsea House World Wide Web address is www.chelseahouse.com

Printed and bound in the United States of America.

9 8 7 6 5 4 3 2

Library of Congress Cataloging-in-Publication Data
Koestler-Grack, Rachel A., 1973–
The story of Clara Barton / by Rachel A. Koestler-Grack.
    p. cm. — (Breakthrough biographies)
Summary: Describes the life of the nurse who served on the battlefields of the Civil War and
later founded the American Red Cross.
Includes bibliographical references and index. 3/06
    ISBN 0-7910-7312-2 3279 8315 3/06
1. Barton, Clara, 1821–1912— Juvenile literature. 2. Red Cross— Biography— Juvenile literature.
3. Nurses—United States— Biography— Juvenile literature. [1. Barton, Clara, 1821–1912. 2. Nurses.
3. Women— Biography.] I. Title. II. Series.
    HV569.B3K64 2004
    361.7′634′092— dc21   2003000267

Selected Sources

Barton, Clara. *The Story of My Childhood.* New York: Arno Press, 1980.

National Park Service. *Clara Barton: Clara Barton National Historic Site.* Washington, D.C.: The
    Division, 1981.

Oates, Stephen B. *A Woman of Valor: Clara Barton and the Civil War.* New York: The Free Press, 1994.

Pryor, Elizabeth Brown. *Clara Barton: Professional Angel.* Philadelphia: University of Pennsylvania
    Press, 1987.

Editorial Credits

Colleen Sexton, editor; Takeshi Takahashi, designer; Mary Englar, photo researcher

Content Reviewer

Susan Finta, National Park Service, Clara Barton National Historic Site, Glen Echo, Maryland

Photo Credits

Library of Congress: cover, 4, 7, 9, 10, 21, 29 (Susan B. Anthony); Corbis: 5, 23, 27; Clara Barton
Birthplace Museum: 8, 17; Clara Barton National Historic Site: 11, 20, 26; Lee Snider/Corbis: 12;
Bettmann/Corbis: title page, 15, 18, 19, 29 (Dorothea Dix and Florence Nightingale); North Wind
Picture Archives: 16; Historical Society of Pennsylvania: 24; Richard T. Nowitz/Corbis: 25; Louisa May
Alcott Memorial Association: 29 (Louisa May Alcott); Stowe-Day Foundation: 29 (Harriet Beecher
Stowe); Rick Apitz: back cover.

Table of Contents

As the Bullets Whizzed By

On September 17, 1862, Clara Barton jumped from her horse-drawn wagon at a battlefield near Antietam Creek in Maryland. A smoky haze and the burning smell of gunpowder filled the air. All around her, Clara heard gunshots and sometimes the pounding of cannons. Through the haze, she saw dozens of wounded, bleeding soldiers lying on the battlefield. Without fear, Clara moved from soldier to soldier, giving them pieces of bread and fresh water. She gently washed and bandaged their wounds as best she could.

During the Civil War, Clara Barton made it her mission to help wounded and suffering soldiers.

Northern and Southern soldiers clash in the Battle of Antietam, the bloodiest battle of the Civil War. Clara nursed some of the 19,000 men wounded in this fierce fight.

One man called to Clara for a drink of water. She rushed to his side and lifted his head. At that moment, a bullet whizzed toward them. She later remembered, "A bullet sped its full and easy way between us, tearing a hole in my sleeve and found its way into his body. He fell back dead."

People of that time doubted that women could work on the front lines of the war. But Clara Barton proved them wrong. She was a strong and brave presence on the battlefields during the Civil War (1861–1865). Throughout this long fight between the Northern states and the Southern states, Clara brought aid to suffering soldiers. She believed it her duty to help all people and to serve her country faithfully. And she would spend her life doing just that.

> "I may be compelled to face danger, but never fear it, and while our soldiers can stand and fight, I can stand and feed and nurse them."
> —Clara Barton

Life on the Farm

On Christmas Day, 1821, the Barton household bustled with excitement. Stephen and Sarah Barton had just had a baby girl. They named their dark-eyed daughter Clarissa Harlowe Barton. As a child, she had the nickname "Tot." But as a young woman, she shortened Clarissa to Clara.

Clara grew up on the family farm in North Oxford, Massachusetts. Her two brothers and two sisters were much older than Clara. They were eager to teach her what they knew best. As soon as she could talk, Clara's oldest brother, Stephen Jr., gave Clara math lessons. Her oldest sister, Dorothea, taught Clara to read. Sally taught Clara **geography,** which became one of her favorite subjects. Best of all, Clara's brother David gave her horseback riding lessons. She loved to gallop around the farm.

> *"I had no playmates, but in effect six fathers and mothers. They were a family of schoolteachers."*
> —Clara Barton

Clara started school just before her fourth birthday. She told her teacher that she could spell "artichoke" and other hard words. He was so impressed that he started her in the advanced reading class. Clara earned excellent grades. But she was very shy and had a hard time getting to know her classmates.

Clara was born on this farm in North Oxford, Massachusetts. Her father built the family's home with his own hands.

Clara remembers listening breathlessly as her father, Stephen Barton (left), told stories about his time as a soldier. Clara's mother, Sarah Barton (right), gave her daughter lessons in cooking, sewing, and keeping house. Clara admired her mother's common sense.

Clara's family worried about her shyness. When she was 8 years old, her parents decided to send her away to boarding school. They hoped a new place and new friends would help her. Clara did very well with her schoolwork. But she kept to herself, fearful that her schoolmates would laugh at her if she made a mistake. Clara left school before the first term ended and continued her studies at home. "I was in constant dread of doing something wrong," she later wrote of her experience at boarding school.

Child Nurse

When Clara was 11 years old, her brother David was helping to build a new barn and fell off the roof. At first, he seemed unhurt. But soon after the fall, David became very ill. Doctors didn't know what was wrong with him. The Bartons feared David's illness was hopeless.

Clara wouldn't give up on her brother. For two years, she nursed David. During this time, she bathed him, fed him, and gave him medicine. She even learned to apply slimy black leeches to his skin. A common cure at that time, the leeches sucked out what was considered "bad blood."

Clara seldom left David's bedside. He finally recovered and knew he owed his life to his little sister. Clara later recalled, "I was the accepted and acknowledged nurse of a man almost too ill to recover." From that time on, she became known for her abilities to care for people.

When Clara's brother David (above) became ill, she helped nurse him back to health. It was during this time that Clara discovered her gift for helping people in need.

A Generous Teacher

As she grew up, Clara found great satisfaction in serving others. She often tutored poor children and cared for people who were sick. Clara's family saw that she was most happy and sure of herself when she was fighting for the good of others. They encouraged her to become a teacher. At age 17, she passed the teaching exam.

In May 1839, Miss Barton arrived at a one-room schoolhouse in North Oxford for her first day as a teacher. She was nervous and scared. But her love of learning excited the students. Her school was named the best-behaved school in town. Clara was surprised and told people she had never spanked or beat her students as other teachers did. She later wrote "Child that I was, I did not know that the surest test of **discipline** is its absence."

Clara's first teaching job was in a one-room schoolhouse much like this one.

This photograph of Clara was probably taken when she was a student at Clinton Liberal Institute in New York. The school encouraged women to take classes in science and math, subjects usually studied only by men at that time.

By 1850, Clara was becoming restless with teaching. She needed a new challenge. "I decided that I must withdraw and find a school, the object of which should be to teach *me* something," she later wrote. Clara attended the Clinton Liberal Institute in Clinton, New York. She studied hard and learned to live on her own, without her family nearby for support.

After a year of studies, Clara decided to leave Clinton. She stayed with friends in Hightstown, New Jersey, and took a teaching position. Unlike the free schools in Massachusetts, the schools in New Jersey were subscription schools. Parents paid a fee for their children to attend.

Clara started one of the first free public schools in New Jersey. Today, this building is known as the Clara Barton Schoolhouse.

Soon Clara was restless again. In 1852, she decided to move to nearby Bordentown, New Jersey. There, Clara noticed that many children did not attend school at all. Their families could not afford to pay the fees of the subscription schools. Clara decided to open a free public school. She convinced Bordentown's school committee to support it.

On the first day of class, only six students attended Clara's school. She shared her love of geography with them, telling stories about foreign countries and customs. Before long, 200 boys and girls became students at the school. The school committee had to hire more teachers. By the end of the year, 400 more children wanted to attend Clara's free school.

> *"I may sometimes be willing to teach for nothing, but if paid at all, I shall never do a man's work for less than a man's pay."*
>
> —Clara Barton

The school committee was pleased with Clara's success. They decided to build a brand new school to hold all 600 students. They also decided to hire a man to be the principal. Clara was shocked and hurt. After all, she had founded the school. But she was a woman, and many people didn't think a woman could handle a position of such authority.

Clara continued to work at the Bordentown school as the new principal's "female assistant." But she and the principal did not get along well. Clara became nervous and ill. She lost her voice. Barely able to whisper, she decided to resign and try to regain her health. At age 32, Clara was not sure what she would do next.

Battlefield Nurse

One day in February 1854, Miss Clara Barton stepped off a train and onto the muddy streets of Washington, D.C. She hoped the milder air of the nation's capital would help bring back her voice. She spent her days reading at the Library of Congress. And she often visited the Capitol to hear members of Congress **debate** the issues of the day.

The United States had become divided on issues of states' rights and slavery. Many Northerners believed slavery was wrong. It was already outlawed in many Northern states. But plantation owners in the South said they needed slave labor to support their large farms. Southerners believed the states should have the right to make their own laws about slavery and other issues. Northerners thought the **federal** government should make laws for the whole country. Clara became a supporter of the Northern point of view.

> *"When there is no longer a soldier's arm to raise the Stars and Stripes above our Capital, may God give strength to mine."*
> —Clara Barton

In July, fully recovered and eager to work, Clara took a job as a clerk in the U.S. Patent Office. With a patent, an inventor became the only person who could make or sell an invention. All day, Clara copied patent applications and rules by hand. Unlike most women of her time, Clara earned the same pay as the male clerks in the office.

Famous photographer Mathew Brady took this photograph of Clara during the Civil War. She earned the respect of foot soldiers and commanders alike. After the war, some soldiers honored her by naming their newborn daughters "Clara."

By 1861, the political situation in the United States was grave. Eleven Southern states had left the Union to form their own government. They called their new country the Confederate States of America. In April 1861, fighting broke out between Union soldiers and Confederate soldiers, starting the Civil War.

Early in the war, Confederate supporters in Baltimore, Maryland, attacked Massachusetts soldiers on their way to Washington, D.C. Three soldiers died and 30 were wounded. Clara joined the crowd gathered to meet the wounded, who arrived in the capital by train. Clara helped care for them and brought them food and supplies. She later recalled, "The **patriot** blood of my fathers was warm in my veins."

Before long, Northern troops had set up camp in Washington, D.C. Clara found the lively bustle of the capital refreshing. She was caught up in the military excitement. In a letter to her father, Clara wrote, "I don't know how long it has been since my ear has been free from the roll of a drum, it is the music I sleep by, and I love it."

Early in the Civil War, 75,000 Union troops set up camp not far from the White House.

there too weak to eat. — a boiled egg for those who could — but most of all the bread and butter, men with shattered limbs, shot through and through — think of them men raised among all the comforts of a Northern home — with the tears of gratitude rolling over their faces at the mere fact of a piece of bread with butter on it. — "Butter Madam I havn't tasted butter in eight months. And to see strong men, manly, educated men, gnawing off the butter side like little children and holding out the ragged slice with poor cold bloody fingers for a little more butter, please," Oh how the gloom of the night wore away, and their poor hearts lightened with only these little helps, and finally as it came day light, and they had slept and

People often wrote to Clara asking about the needs of the soldiers. In this letter, Clara writes back, noting how grateful the men are for just a little butter on their bread.

Clara saw that the War Department was unprepared to support the army camps, so she worked hard to fill this need. She asked citizens, businesses, and charities to donate money and supplies. Soon Clara had filled three warehouses. She desperately wanted to travel to the war's **front,** where she could deliver the supplies and tend to the wounded. But the Union Army felt it was unsafe and unwise for women to be near battlefields. She met with the Union quartermaster, who handed out food and clothing to soldiers. When he heard that Clara had three warehouses full of supplies, he requested a pass to the front for her.

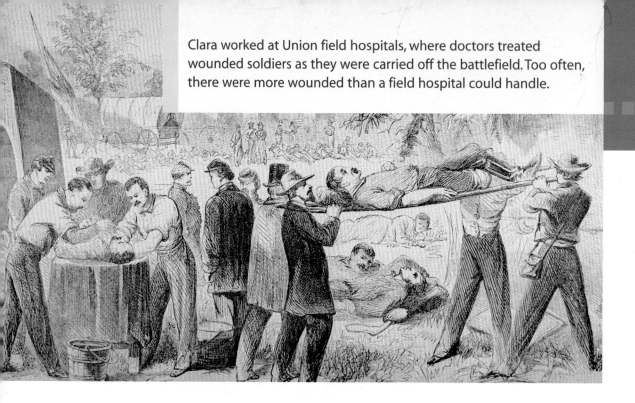

Clara worked at Union field hospitals, where doctors treated wounded soldiers as they were carried off the battlefield. Too often, there were more wounded than a field hospital could handle.

Clara served on the front during much of the war, often with little rest. She brought food and supplies to the battlefields. She fed and cared for thousands of soldiers at a time. There were often more soldiers to feed than she had supplies. She once noted, "two water buckets, 5 tin cups, 1 camp kettle, 1 stewpan, 2 lanterns, 4 bread knives, 3 plates, and a 2-quart tin dish—and 3,000 guests to serve." Clara assisted doctors, bandaged wounds, and comforted soldiers. She also organized teams of nurses to give aid to the wounded. And she bravely faced the dangers of war. "I am a U.S. soldier," Clara told herself, as she marched on foot, dodged bullets, went without food, and slept under the stars.

Perhaps Clara's finest moments of the war came during the Battle of Antietam. She worked tirelessly, assisting doctors, comforting soldiers, and cooking pot after pot of cornmeal gruel. Clara even performed surgery, removing a bullet from a soldier's cheekbone. At Antietam, she showed everyone her skills and her courage. It was during this battle that Clara Barton gained the undying admiration and respect of doctors, soldiers, and the army itself.

Firsts for Women

In the 1800s, women had few rights. They could not vote, and in some areas they could not own property. In most places, women could not go to college and could hold only certain jobs, such as cook, launderer, or teacher. Even in these jobs, women were not paid much for their work. And they often received less pay than men who did the same job.

Many women were trying to break through these barriers. They knew they deserved the same rights as men. They wanted to learn, work, and earn money, just as men did. And they wanted to be paid the same as men for the same work.

The 1800s saw many firsts for women. In 1837, Mary Lyon founded Mount Holyoke College, the first women's college in the United States. In 1849, Elizabeth Blackwell was the first woman to earn a medical degree. Lucy Hobbs Taylor became the first woman dentist in 1866. In 1887, Susanna Salter of Argonia, Kansas, was the first woman elected mayor. Women also established the American Woman Suffrage Association in 1869. This group would eventually help women win the right to vote in 1920.

Throughout the 1800s and early 1900s, women spoke out for the right to vote. In 1920, the 19th Amendment to the Constitution granted voting rights to all women in America.

The Search for Missing Soldiers

The Civil War drew to an end in the spring of 1865, with the North claiming victory. But Clara knew she couldn't go back to her quiet life. She needed to help others. Thousands of soldiers were missing. Many were prisoners. Others had died or left the army to start a new life. Clara decided to ask President Abraham Lincoln if she could help families find their loved ones. He agreed and wrote her a letter that was published in newspapers. It said all requests for information about missing soldiers should be sent to Miss Clara Barton.

Clara set up an office in Annapolis, Maryland. She received more than 100 requests a day. Soon Clara had a list of more than 20,000 names. She regularly published the list in newspapers and mailed it to post offices. When she learned information about a soldier on the list, she contacted his family.

During Clara's visit to Andersonville Prison, there was a ceremony to honor the Union soldiers who had died there. Clara raised the American flag. When the small crowd began singing "The Star-Spangled Banner," she wept.

A poster advertises one of Clara's popular lectures. She spoke as many as 14 times a month and earned $75 to $100 for each lecture. These funds helped Clara continue her work searching for missing soldiers.

LECTURE!

MISS CLARA BARTON,

OF WASHINGTON,

THE HEROINE OF ANDERSONVILLE,

The Soldier's Friend, who gave her time and fortune during the war to the Union cause, and who is now engaged in searching for the missing soldiers of the Union army, will address the people of

LAMBERTVILLE, in

HOLCOMBE HALL,

THIS EVENING,

APRIL 7TH, AT 7½ O'CLOCK.

SUBJECT:

SCENES ON THE BATTLE-FIELD.

ADMISSION,   25 CENTS.

The Secretary of War asked Clara to travel to Andersonville Prison in Georgia. Many Union soldiers had died from poor conditions in this Confederate prison. They had been buried in graves marked only with numbers. A Union prisoner had kept a list that matched names to the numbers. Using this information, Clara helped identify almost 12,500 soldiers who were listed as missing.

Early in 1866, Clara persuaded government officials to award her a $15,000 **grant** to help continue her work. Around the same time, a friend suggested that Clara raise money by giving speeches about her war experiences. Her old feelings of shyness returned. Clara wrote, "I would rather stand behind the lines of artillery at Antietam, or cross the pontoon bridge under fire at Fredericksburg, than to be expected to preside at a public meeting." But she agreed to try. During the next two years, she traveled the country, telling stories of the war to eager crowds.

Founding the American Red Cross

By the spring of 1869, Clara was worn out. After two years of traveling and speeches, she needed to rest. She decided to take a trip to Europe, where she could visit friends and regain her health.

In Switzerland, Clara learned about the Geneva Convention of 1864. At this meeting, 12 countries signed a **treaty.** This document made rules for the treatment of wounded soldiers and prisoners of war. It set up an organization called the Red Cross that would take no sides in a war. Its only job was to help people who were suffering.

During her time in Europe, Clara found it difficult to rest. When the Franco-Prussian War broke out in July 1870, Clara volunteered for the Red Cross. Warehouses filled with supplies and the organization of the workers impressed her. She wrote that the Red Cross workers were "accomplishing in four months under their systematic organization what we failed to accomplish in four years." She told herself, "If I live to return to my country, I will try to make my people understand the Red Cross and that treaty."

> *"In time of peace and prosperity, prepare for war and calamity."*
>
> —Motto of the International Red Cross

In 1873, Clara went home to the United States. By 1876, she had begun the fight to bring the Red Cross to America. She discovered that government officials did not want to sign the treaty because the Red Cross supported wartime

Clara worked hard to bring the Red Cross to the United States. She showed government officials how the organization could help people during peacetime, as well as during war.

emergencies. Americans were tired of war and didn't want to aid any wars in Europe. But Clara convinced officials that the Red Cross could help during floods, hurricanes, earthquakes, and other peacetime emergencies. In March 1882, Congress passed the Treaty of Geneva, making the United States part of the international program. It was one of Clara Barton's greatest accomplishments.

In 1889, a flood in Johnstown, Pennsylvania, swept away parts of the town and killed more than 2,000 people. Clara brought the Red Cross to Johnstown to help those who were left homeless and in need of food, clothing, and medicine.

At age 59, Clara was the first president of the American Red Cross. The Red Cross helped communities all over the country. Workers delivered food, clothing, and medicine to people in need of aid. Newspapers praised the efforts of the Red Cross, and the group soon gained great national support. Clara asked for donations of money and supplies. She also organized work groups, kept records, and set up **relief** efforts. Clara even traveled to aid people in other countries.

Clara was proud of her work with the Red Cross. During her years as president, she had made a difference in thousands of lives. But some people did not agree that Clara was a good leader. They thought she had too much control and kept poor records. Some people thought she was too old to be in charge. But Clara wouldn't give up. She wanted to leave the Red Cross only when she was ready. In 1897, she moved to Glen Echo, Maryland, and ran the Red Cross headquarters from there. It wasn't until 1904, at age 82, that Clara finally decided to resign. The Red Cross then moved its offices to Washington, D.C.

The American Red Cross Today

Every year, the American Red Cross responds to thousands of disasters and emergencies across the United States. Workers rush quickly to the scenes of fires, floods, hurricanes, tornadoes, and earthquakes. They also travel to places where explosions, chemical spills, or accidents have happened. Red Cross workers give victims shelter, food, and medical care. They also help people return to their normal way of life after a disaster. The Red Cross runs a blood program, too. Workers collect, store, and give out blood when injured or sick people need it.

The American Red Cross is not part of the government. But Congress gave it a **charter,** or the power and responsibility to provide aid during disasters. The president of the United States is the honorary chairperson and names the American Red Cross's leader. The Red Cross gives aid for free. People volunteer or give money to the Red Cross to support its work. Ever since Clara Barton started the Red Cross in the United States, it has followed its mission to help people in need.

Completed in 1917, the American Red Cross National Headquarters stands in Washington, D.C. The building also serves as a memorial to the heroic women of the Civil War.

Clara spent her final years in Glen Echo, but she didn't stop working for the good of others. In 1905, she founded the National First Aid Association of America, saying "another work reaches out its hands to me and I have taken them." Until 1910, she served as honorary president of the group, which taught people about first aid and how to prepare for emergencies.

On April 12, 1912, Clara died of double pneumonia at age 90. Today we remember her as a great **humanitarian,** a woman committed to service. She overcame her shy nature to fight battle after battle for the lives of others. By founding the American Red Cross, Clara Barton made sure her mission to help people in need would continue for generations.

This house in Glen Echo, Maryland, was Clara's home and the first headquarters of the American Red Cross. Today, the house serves as the Clara Barton National Historic Site.

Clara Barton was one of the most important women in American history. Through her work as a teacher, nurse, and humanitarian, she made a difference in thousands of lives.

Did You Know?

- Clara became known as "The Angel of the Battlefield" for her service during the Civil War.

- In 1883, Clara worked for six months as the female superintendent of a women's prison in Massachusetts.

- Clara became the first woman sent as a **diplomat** from the United States when she attended the Third International Conference of the Red Cross in 1884.

- The International Red Cross changed the Geneva Treaty to include peacetime emergencies as Clara had done in the United States. To honor her, they named the change the American Amendment.

- Clara often spoke out for women's rights and woman suffrage, or the right of women to vote. She was a speaker at the First International Woman Suffrage Conference in 1888.

- Clara received many letters from children who wanted to know more about her life. But she couldn't answer all the letters. Instead, Clara wrote an autobiography called *The Story of My Childhood*.

Important Dates

December 25, 1821: Clara Barton is born in North Oxford, Massachusetts.

1830: Clara is sent to boarding school; she returns home before the end of the term.

1839: Clara becomes a teacher in North Oxford. (age 17)

1850–1851: Clara attends Clinton Liberal Institute in New York.

1852: Clara opens New Jersey's first free public school in Bordentown.

1854: Clara moves to Washington, D.C., and finds a job at the U.S. Patent Office. (age 32)

April 12, 1861: The Civil War begins.

April 19, 1861: Massachusetts soldiers on their way to Washington, D.C., are attacked by mobs in Baltimore, Maryland; Clara cares for the wounded and starts gathering supplies.

August 3, 1862: Clara gains permission to work on the battlefields. (age 40)

September 17, 1862: Battle of Antietam

March, 1865: President Abraham Lincoln gives Clara his support to find missing soldiers.

April 9, 1865: The Civil War ends.

Summer, 1865: Clara goes to Andersonville Prison in Georgia, where she identifies the graves of 12,500 soldiers listed as missing.

1866–1868: Clara gives speeches about her Civil War experiences.

1869: Clara travels to Europe, where she learns about the International Red Cross. (age 47)

March 16, 1882: President Chester A. Arthur signs the Treaty of Geneva; the United States joins the International Red Cross; Clara becomes president of the American Red Cross. (age 60)

1904: Clara resigns as president of the American Red Cross. (age 82)

April 12, 1912: Clara dies at her home in Glen Echo, Maryland. (age 90)

Louisa May Alcott (1832–1888)
Best known for her book *Little Women*, Alcott also served as a nurse during the Civil War. She later wrote a first-hand account of her wartime experiences called *Hospital Sketches*.

Susan B. Anthony (1820–1906)
Anthony was a strong and dedicated leader of the women's rights movement. Like Clara Barton, Anthony believed women should have the same opportunities as men did, including the right to vote. Anthony and Clara met after the Civil War. Anthony encouraged Clara's support of the woman suffrage movement.

Dorothea Dix (1802–1887)
During the Civil War, Dix became the Union's Superintendent of Female Nurses. She set up a nursing corps to care for wounded and sick soldiers. When Dix hired new nurses, she chose only women who were "plain looking" and more than 30 years old. She felt these women would be serious about nursing, would work hard, and would not faint at the sight of blood.

Florence Nightingale (1820–1910)
Nightingale was a British nurse. During the Crimean War (1854–1856) in Turkey, she served as the head of nursing operations. Like Clara Barton, Florence Nightingale publicly spoke out against poor sanitary and medical conditions for wounded soldiers. Her efforts helped reduce deaths during the war.

Harriet Beecher Stowe (1811–1896)
Stowe became famous for writing *Uncle Tom's Cabin*, a story that showed the terrible treatment of slaves in the South. The book inspired many people to fight for the freedom of slaves. Some people think it helped start the Civil War. Clara Barton greatly admired the book and gave it to her students to read.

Glossary

charter (CHAR-tuhr) a document that states the rights or duties of a group of people; the U.S. Congress gave the American Red Cross a charter in 1905.

debate (dih-BAYT) to discuss all sides of an issue; members of Congress had long debates over the issues of states' rights and slavery in the years leading up to the Civil War.

diplomat (DIP-luh-mat) a person who represents his or her country's government in another country

discipline (DISS-uh-plin) to control the way someone behaves; Clara believed that showing kindness and respect to people made them behave well.

federal (FED-uhr-uhl) a central power or authority; the federal government in the United States includes Congress, which makes laws for the whole country.

front (FRUHNT) the place where armies fight battles; Clara believed she could give the best help to wounded soldiers on the battlefield.

geography (jee-AHG-ruh-fee) the study of the earth, including its land forms, people, climates, and resources; as a child, Clara loved geography and spent many hours tracing rivers, oceans, and countries on a map.

grant (GRANT) money given by the government or an organization to be used for a special purpose

humanitarian (hyoo-man-uh-TAYR-ee-uhn) a person who stands up for the well-being of other people; Clara is known as a humanitarian for her dedication to education, nursing, and women's rights.

patriot (PAY-tree-uht) someone who loves his or her country

relief (rih-LEEF) aid given to people who are suffering or in need

treaty (TREE-tee) an agreement between two or more countries

To Learn More

READ THESE BOOKS

Nonfiction

Chang, Ina. *A Separate Battle: Women and the Civil War.* New York: Puffin Books, 1996.

Francis, Dorothy Brenner. *Clara Barton: Founder of the American Red Cross.* Brookfield, Conn.: Millbrook Press, 2002.

Ray, Delia. *A Nation Torn: The Story of How the Civil War Began.* New York: Penguin Putnam, 1996.

Whitelaw, Nancy. *Clara Barton: Civil War Nurse.* Springfield, N.J.: Enslow, 1997.

Fiction

Hunt, Irene. *Across Five Aprils.* Morristown, N.J.: Silver Burdett Press, 1993.

Shura, Mary Francis. *Gentle Annie: The True Story of a Civil War Nurse.* New York: Scholastic Press, 1991.

LOOK UP THESE INTERNET SITES

American Red Cross Museum
www.redcross.org/museum
Learn about the history of the American Red Cross through articles, photographs, and time lines.

Clara Barton National Historic Site
www.nps.gov/clba/
Click on "In Depth" to learn more about Clara's Glen Echo house, view a photo gallery, and read a chronology of her life.

Clara Barton's Pages
www.geocities.com/Athens/Aegean/6732/cb.html
Read a biography of Clara Barton, see places where she lived and worked, and read her poem, "The Women Who Went to the Field."

A Nation Divided: The U.S. Civil War 1861-1865
www.historyplace.com/civilwar/
Learn about the Civil War by following a time line of its major battles and events.

Internet search key words: Clara Barton, Civil War, Battle of Antietam, Civil War Women, American Red Cross

Index